PARADES OF ARRAYS

Mel Campbell

Rourke

Publishing LLC
Vero Beach, Florida 32964

www.rourkepublishing.com

PHOTO CREDITS: © Alex Preiss: title page; © Jeffrey Smit: page 4; © Georgios Alexandris: page 5; © Matthew Hull: page 9; © Lisa McDonald: page 21; © Kenneth O'Quinn: page 22

Editor: Robert Stengard-Olliges

Cover design by Nicola Stratford.

Library of Congress Cataloging-in-Publication Data

Campbell, Mel.
  Parades of arrays / Mel Campbell.
     p. cm.
  Includes index.
  ISBN 1-59515-980-0 (hardcover)
  ISBN 1-59515-951-7 (paperback)
  1. Counting--Juvenile literature. 2. Arithmetic--Juvenile literature. 3.
Orthogonal arrays--Juvenile literature. 4. Parades--Juvenile literature.
I. Title.
  QA113.C352 2007
  513.2'11--dc22
                                            2006019792

Printed in the USA

CG/CG

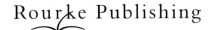

Rourke Publishing

www.rourkepublishing.com – sales@rourkepublishing.com
Post Office Box 3328, Vero Beach, FL 32964

TABLE OF CONTENTS

PARADE DAY

Dad and Tom were up early. It was the day of the big **parade**.

Dad called it the day of the Parades of **Arrays**!
Tom asked, "What is an array, Dad?"
Dad answered, "An array is made up of **columns** and
rows. Look at these soldiers marching in columns
and rows."

COLUMNS AND ROWS

    Tom didn't know that the parade that he and his Dad were going to would be filled with arrays. Tom thought about columns and rows and arrays. He thought that this would be a strange parade.

After Dad parked the car they found a place on a hillside to sit and watch the parade.

They would be able to see the entire parade coming down the street. Tom was still thinking about columns and rows.

"Here comes the marching band," shouted Tom.
"Do you see any columns and rows?" asked Dad.

Tom was not sure. So Dad took out a paper and pencil and made a **sketch** of 3 columns and 4 rows of stars.

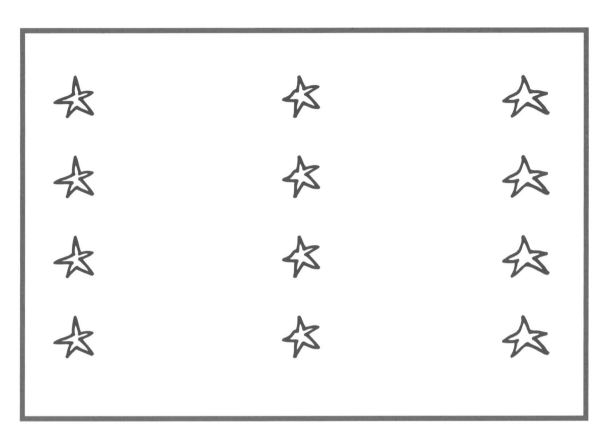

3+3+3+3=12

4+4+4=12

3 x 4=12

4 x 3=12

In the sky, old military planes flew over the parade.

"Dad, look at those old planes! They are in columns and rows too."

There were 2 columns of 3 rows of planes. Tom counted six of those old planes.

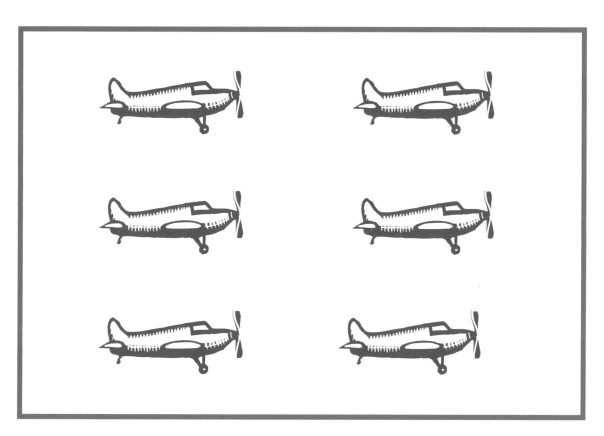

2+2+2=6

3+3=6

2 x 3=6

3 x 2=6

BICYCLES AND CLOWNS

Next in the parade was a group riding bicycles in columns and rows. Tom counted twelve of them. He saw there were 3 columns and 4 rows.

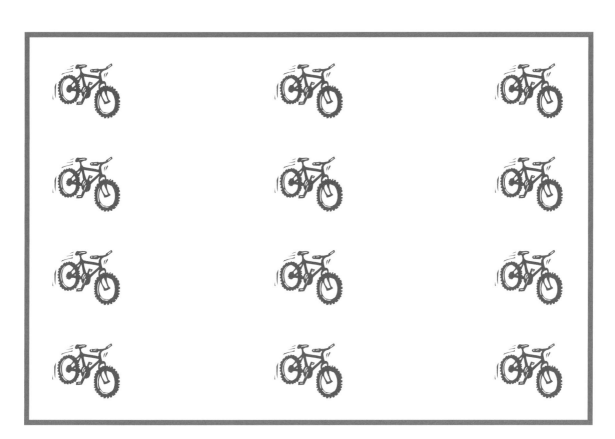

3+3+3+3=12

4+4+4=12

3 x 4=12

4 x 3=12

Tom had just finished counting the bicycle riders when the clowns appeared.

"There are 25 clowns! I have never seen so many clowns in one place."

"Dad, is that an array of clowns?"

"Yes Tom, that is an array of clowns."

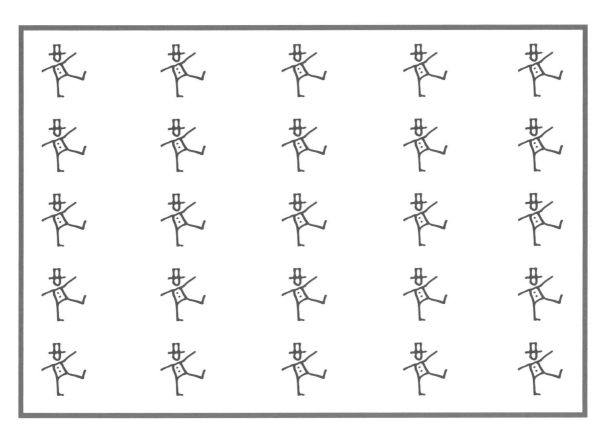

5+5+5+5+5=25

5 x 5=25

HORSES TOO

By now Tom knew what an array was and why Dad called it a Parade of Arrays. After the clowns there was an array of horses. Tom could see there were 7 columns and 3 rows of horses. He counted 21 horses.

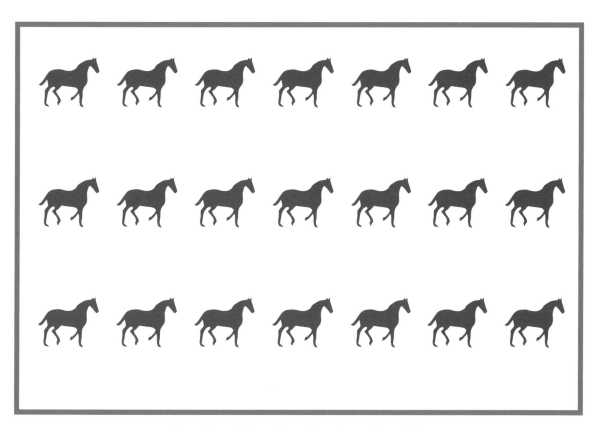

3+3+3+3+3+3+3=21

7+7+7=21

7 x 3=21

3 x 7=21

Well that was the end of the parade and Tom was all smiles. Now he knew a lot about arrays!

Tom could see arrays in lots of things, even things in his home. There was the tile floor in his kitchen in columns and rows.

The stars on the flag were in columns and rows. Tom said quietly to himself, "Hurray for arrays!"

Glossary

array (uh RAY) — ordering sets in rows and columns to make it easier to count

columns (KOL uhm) — vertical groups

parade (puh RADE) — organized procession of people in a street

row (ROH) — horizontal group

sketch (SKECH) — a quick drawing

Index

Further Reading

Amato, William. *Math on the Playground.* Children's Press, 2002.
Beers, Bonnie. *Everyone Uses Math.* Yellow Umbrella Books, 2002.
Tang, Greg. *The Grapes of Math.* Scholastic, 2004.

Websites To Visit

www.figurethis.org
www.mathcats.com
ksnn.larc.nasa.gov/k2/k2_math.htm

About The Author

In addition to his work as an university education professor, Melvin Campbell can often be found in elementary classrooms sharing his love for words in creative and dramatic ways. Dr. Campbell enjoys collecting maps and along with his wife is an avid bird watcher.